Pawfect

FRIENDS

Pawfect FRIENDS

JACK RUSSELL

amber
BOOKS

Published by
Amber Books Ltd
United House
North Road
London
N7 9DP
United Kingdom
www.amberbooks.co.uk
Appstore: itunes.com/apps/amberbooksltd
Facebook: www.facebook.com/amberbooks
Twitter: @amberbooks

ISBN: 978-1-78274-586-0

Project Editor: Sarah Uttridge
Designer: Keren Harragan
Picture Research: Terry Forshaw

Printed in China

PICTURE CREDITS
Depositphotos: 23 (Vvvita), 26 (Lilun Li), 27 (Belchonock), 30 (snb2087), 31 (Gurinaleksander), 33 (Belchonock)

Dreamstime: 6 (Lulya), 7 (Gurinaleksander), 8 (Krivitskaia), 9 (Donna Kilday), 10 (Natalia Bachkova), 12 (Dragonika), 13 (Ksoloits), 15 (Gurinaleksander), 16 (Onetouchspark), 18 (Tomasz Wrzesien), 19 (Szilvia Papkutasi), 20 (Cynoclub), 21 (Dennis van de Water), 22 (Lilun Li), 24 (Oleksandr Lytvynenko), 25 (Vladimir Suponev), 29 (Creativefire), 32 (Vvvita), 35 (Satit Srihin), 36 (Petar Dojkic), 38 (Tzooka), 39 (Vladimir Suponev), 40 (Michael Bednarek), 41 (Beck Lilia), 42 (Mitja Mladkovic), 43 (Jiori Vaclavek), 46 (Lilun Li), 47 (Justvrins), 48 (Erik Lam), 49 (Adrian Garneata), 50 (Nagy-Bagoly Ilona), 51 (Julija Sapic), 52 (Williecole), 53 (Vasyl Helevachuk), 56 (Adogslifephoto), 57 (Nagy-Bagoly Ilona), 58 (Bokstaz), 59 (Virgilijus Bumbulis), 60 (Lilun), 62 (De Jongh), 64 (Adogslifephoto), 65 & 66 (Lilun Li), 70 (Elena Vasilchenko), 71 (De Jongh), 73 (Konstantin Tavrov), 74 (Casfotoarda), 76 (Amy Overholt), 78 (Anna Krivitskaia), 82 (Vino), 83 (Onetouchspark), 84 (Cynoclub), 89 (Jiri Vaclavek), 90 (Leboa1), 91 (Gurnaleskander), 92 (Onetouchspark), 94 (Ksoloits), 95 (Vvvita)

Dreamstime/Photodeti: 5, 11, 14, 17, 28, 34, 37, 44, 45, 63, 67, 68, 69, 72, 75, 77, 79, 80, 81, 85, 86, 87, 88, 93, 96

Fotolia: 55 (Africa Studio)

Shutterstock: 54 (Irina Kozorog), 61 (Alessandro Pinto)

Pawfect Friends

As the saying almost goes: cats and dogs that eat together, stay together. Or was it those that share a blanket? Or a laundry basket? Well, whether it is dining or slumbering together, going for walks together, following each other around the garden or even giving piggyback rides; whether it is old cats with young pups or ageing hounds with kittens, here are some of the sweetest buddies imaginable.